Ruysbroeck and the Mystics

with selections from Ruysbroeck
(Large Print Edition)

Maurice Maeterlinck

translated by
Jane T. Stoddart

Contents

M. Maeterlinck's introduction to his translation of "The Adornment of the Spiritual Marriage."

I	9
II	24

Selected passages from "The Adornment of the Spiritual Marriage."

On the Kingdom of the Soul	77
Christ the Sun of the Soul	80
The Lesson from the Bee	82
The Dew of Mid-day	84
The Lesson from the Ant	86
What shall the Forsaken do?	88
The Setting of the Eternal Sun	90
The Nature of God	92
The Divine Generosity	93
Christ the Lover of all Men	95
How Christ gave Himself to us in the Sacrament	97

The Soul's Hunger for God   100
The Labour and Rest of Love   102
The Christian Life   103
The Coming of the Bridegroom   104

Reviews of precedent Editions   107

Translator's Note

The following is an authorised translation of the essay prefixed by M. Maeterlinck to *L'Ornement des Noces Spirituelles*, de *Ruysbroeck L'Admirable*, Traduit du Flamand par Maurice Maeterlinck, which was published in 1891 by Paul Lacomblez of Brussels. I have added selected passages from Ruysbroeck's own work.

Jane T. Stoddart

The Mystic Jan van Ruysbroek by Antony van der Does

M. Maeterlinck's introduction to his translation of "The Adornment of the Spiritual Marriage."

I

Many works are more correctly beautiful than this book of Ruysbroeck L'Admirable. Many mystics—Swedenborg and Novalis among others—are more potent in their influence, and more timely. It is very probable that his writings may but rarely meet the needs of to-day. Looking at him from another point of view, I know few more clumsy authors. He wanders off now and then into strange puerilities, and the first twenty chapters of *The Adornment of the Spiritual Marriage*, although they are perhaps a necessary preparation for what follows, contain little more than mild and pious commonplaces. Outwardly, at least, he has no order, no logic of the schools. He is full of repetitions, and sometimes seems to contradict himself. He shows the ignorance of a child along with the wisdom of one who might have returned from the dead. Over his involved syntax I have toiled more than once in the sweat of my brow. He introduces an image, and forgets it. There are some of his images which the mind cannot realise, and this phenomenon, so unusual in an honest work, can only be explained by his awkwardness or his extraordinary haste. He knows few of the tricks of language, and can speak only of the unspeakable. He is almost entirely ignorant of the habits, skilled methods, and resources of philosophic thought, and he is constrained to think only of the unthinkable. When he speaks of his little monastic garden, he can hardly tell us enough about what goes on there; on that subject he writes like a child. He undertakes to teach us what transpires in the nature of God, and writes pages which Plato could not have written. Everywhere we find a grotesque disproportion between his knowledge and ignorance, his capacity and desire. You must not expect a literary work; you will see only the convulsive flight of an eagle, dizzy, blind, and wounded, over snowy peaks. I will add one word more by way of friendly warning. It has been my lot to read books generally considered most abstruse: *The Disciples at Saïs*, and the *Fragments* of Novalis, for instance; the *Biographia Literaria* and the *Friend* of Samuel Taylor Coleridge; the *Timaeus* of Plato; the *Enneads* of Plotinus; the *Divine Names* of St. Denys the Areopagite; the *Aurora* of the great German mystic, Jacob Böhme, with whom our author has more than one point of analogy. I do not venture to say that the works of Ruysbroeck are more abstruse than these works; but their abstruseness is less readily pardoned, because we have here to do with an unknown writer in whom we have no previous confidence. I thought it necessary to give an honest warning to idlers on the threshold of this temple without architecture; for this translation was undertaken only to please a few Platonists. I believe that those who have not lived in close fellowship with Plato and with the Neo-Platonists of Alexandria will not proceed far in reading it. They will think they are entering the void; they will feel as if they were falling steadily into a bottomless abyss, between black and slippery rocks. In this book there is no common light or air; as a spiritual abode it will be insupportable to those who come unprepared. Do not enter here from literary curiosity; there are hardly any dainty nicknacks, and the botanist in search of fine images will find as few flowers here as on the polar ice-banks. I tell them that this is a boundless desert, where they will die of thirst. They will find here very few phrases which one may handle and admire after the way of literary critics; nothing but jets of flame or blocks of ice. Do not seek for roses in Iceland. Some flower may still linger between two icebergs—and indeed there are strange outbursts, unknown expressions, unheard-of analogies, but they will not repay you for the time lost in coming so far to pluck them. Before entering here one must be in a philosophic state as different from our ordinary condition as the state of waking is from that of slumber. Porphyry, in his *Principles of the Theory of Intelligibles*, seems to me to have written a warning which might fitly stand at the beginning of this book—"By our intelligence we say many things of the principle which is higher than the intelligence. But these things are divined much better by an absence of thought than by thought. It is the same with this idea as with that of sleep, of which we speak up to a certain point in our waking state, but the knowledge and perception of which we can gain only by sleeping. Like is known only by like, and the condition of all knowledge is that the subject should become like to the object."

It is most difficult, I repeat, to understand such things without preparation; and I believe that, in spite of our preparatory studies, a great deal of this mysticism will seem to us purely theoretic, and that the most of these experiences of supernatural psychology will be accessible to us only in the character of spectators. The philosophical imagination is a faculty which is educated very slowly. We are here, all at once, on the confines of human thought, and far within the polar circle of the mind. It is strangely cold here; it is strangely dark; and yet all around there is light and flame. But to those who come without having trained their mind to these new perceptions, this light and these flames are as dark and cold as painted images. We are dealing here with the most exact of sciences. We have to explore the most rugged and least habitable promontories of the divine "Know Thyself"; and the midnight sun hangs over the tempestuous sea, where the psychology of man mingles with the psychology of God. We have constantly to keep in mind that we are dealing here with a very profound science, and not with a dream. Dreams are not unanimous; dreams have no roots; while the glowing flower of divine metaphysic, which is here full blown, has its mysterious roots in Persia and in India, in Egypt and in Greece. And yet it seems unconscious as a flower, and knows nothing of its roots. Unhappily it is almost impossible for us to put ourselves in the position of the soul which, without effort, conceived this science; we cannot perceive it *ab intra* and reproduce it in ourselves. We lack that which Emerson would call the same "central spontaneity"; we can no longer transform these ideas into our own substance; the utmost we can do is to take count, from the outside, of the tremendous experiences which are within the reach of only a very few souls during the whole existence of a planetary system. "It is not lawful," says Plotinus, "to inquire into the origin of this intuitive science as if it were a thing dependent on place and movement; for it does not approach from here, nor set out from there, in order to go elsewhere, but it appears or does not appear. So that we must not pursue it in order to discover its secret sources, but wait in silence until it suddenly shines out upon us, preparing ourselves for the sacred sight, as the eye waits patiently for the rising of the sun." And elsewhere he adds: "It is not by imagination nor by reason, which is itself obliged to draw its principles from elsewhere, that we represent to ourselves intelligible things (that is to say, the highest of all), but rather it is by our faculty for beholding them, the faculty which enables us to speak of them here below. We see them therefore by awaking in ourselves, here on earth, the same powers which we shall have to awake when we are in the world of pure intelligence. We are like a man who, on reaching the summit of a rock, perceives with his eyes objects which are invisible to those who have not made the ascent along with him."

But although all beings, from the stone and the plant up to man, are contemplations, they are unconscious contemplations; and it is very difficult to rediscover in ourselves some memory of the previous activity of the dead faculty. In this respect we resemble the eye in the Neo-Platonic image. "It turns away from the light to see the darkness, and by the very action it ceases to see; for it cannot see the darkness with the light, and yet without it, it sees not at all; and so, by not seeing, it sees the darkness as far as it is capable of seeing it."

I know the judgment which most men will pronounce on this book. They will think it the work of a deluded monk, of a pale solitary, a hermit, dizzy with fasting and worn with fever. They will take it for a wild, dark dream, crossed with vivid lightning flashes, —nothing more. This is the common idea which people form of the mystics; and they forget too often that they alone are the possessors of certainty. If it be true, as has been said, that every man is a Shakespeare in his dreams, we might well ask whether every man is not in this life an inarticulate mystic, a thousand times more transcendental than those who have confined themselves within the bonds of words. Is not the eye of the lover or of the mother, for instance, a thousand times more abstruse, more impenetrable, and more mystical than this book, which is poor and easily explained, after all, like all books, for these are but dead mysteries, whose horizon will never be rekindled? If we do not understand this, perhaps the reason is that we no longer understand anything. But, to return to our author, a few will recognise without difficulty that, far from being half-maddened by hunger, solitude, and fever, this monk possessed, on the contrary, one of the wisest, most exact, and most subtle philosophic brains which have ever existed. He lived, they tell us, in his hut at Grönendal, in the midst of the forest of Soignes. It was at the beginning of one of the wildest centuries of the middle ages,—the fourteenth. He knew no Greek, and perhaps no Latin. He was alone and poor; and yet, in the depths of this obscure forest of Brabant, his mind, ignorant and simple as it was, receives, all unconsciously, dazzling sunbeams from all the lonely, mysterious peaks of human thought He knows, though he is unaware of it, the Platonism of Greece, the Sufism of Persia, the Brahmanism of India, and the Buddhism of Tibet; and his marvellous ignorance rediscovers the wisdom of buried centuries, and foresees the knowledge of centuries yet unborn. I could quote whole pages of Plato, of Plotinus, of Porphyry, of the Zendic books, of the Gnostics, and of the Kabbala, the all but inspired substance of which is to be found intact in the writings of this humble Flemish priest.[1] We find strange coincidences and disturbing agreements. We find more, for he seems, at times, to have presupposed with exactitude the work of most of his unknown predecessors. Just as Plotinus begins his stern journey at the crossroad where Plato, fearing, paused and knelt down, so we might say that Ruysbroeck awakened from a slumber of several centuries; not, indeed, the same kind of thought (for that kind of thought never sleeps), but the same kind of language as that which had fallen asleep on the mountains where Plotinus forsook it, dazzled by that blaze of light, and with his hands before his eyes, as if in presence of an immense conflagration.

But the organic method of their thought differs strangely. Plato and Plotinus are before all things princes in the sphere of dialectic. They reach mysticism by the science of reasoning. They use the discursive faculties of their mind, and seem to distrust their intuitive or contemplative faculties. Reasoning beholds itself in the mirror of reasoning, and endeavours to remain indifferent to every other reflection. It continues its course like a river of fresh water in the midst of the sea, with the presentiment of a speedy absorption. In our author we find, on the contrary, the habits of Asiatic thought; the intuitive faculty reigns alone above the discursive purification of ideas by means of words. The fetters of the dream have fallen off. Is it for this reason less sure? None can tell. The mirror of the human intellect is entirely unknown in this book, but there is another mirror, darker and more profound, which we hide in the inmost depths of our being; no detail can be seen distinctly, and words will not remain on its surface; the intellect would break it if it could for a moment cast thereon the reflection of its merely secular light; but something else is seen there from time to time. Is it the soul? is it God Himself? is it both at once? We shall never know; yet these all but invisible appearances are the only real rulers of the life of the most unbelieving among us. Here you will perceive nothing but the dark reflections on the mirror, and, as its treasure is inexhaustible, these reflections are not like anything we have experienced in ourselves, but, in spite of all, they have an amazing certainty. And this is why I know nothing more terrifying than this honest book. There is no psychological idea, no metaphysical experience, no mystical intuition, however abstruse, profound, and surprising they may be, which it would be impossible to reproduce if necessary, and to cause to live for a moment in ourselves, that we might be assured of their human identity; but here on earth we are like a blind father who can no longer recall the faces of his children. None of these thoughts has the childlike or brotherly look of a thought of this earth; we seem to have lost our experience of God, and yet everything assures us that we are not entered into the house of dreams. Must we exclaim with Novalis that the time has passed away when the Spirit of God was comprehensible, and that the divine sense of the world is forever lost? That of old all things were manifestations of the Spirit, but that now we see only lifeless reflections which we do not understand, and live entirely on the fruits of better times?

I believe we must humbly confess that the key of this book is not to be found on the common pathways of the human mind. That key is not meant to open earthly doors, and we must deserve it by withdrawing ourselves as far as possible from the earth. One guide, indeed, we may still meet at these lonely cross-roads, who can point out the last way-marks towards these mysterious isles of fire, these Icelands of abstraction and of love. That guide is Plotinus, who attempted to analyse, by means of the human intellect, the divine faculty which here holds sway. He experienced the same ecstasies (as we say in a word which explains nothing) which are in their essence only the beginning of the complete discovery of our being; and in the midst of their trouble and their darkness, he never for one moment closed the questioning eye of the psychologist who seeks to explain to himself the most abnormal phenomena of his soul. He is thus like the last outwork of the pier, from which we may understand something of the waves and the horizon of that dim sea. He tries to extend the paths of the ordinary intellect into the very heart of these desolations, and this is why we must constantly revert to him, for he is the one analytical mystic. For the sake of those who may be tempted to undertake this tremendous journey, I give here one of the pages in which he has attempted to explain the organism of that divine faculty of introspection:—

"In the intuition of the intellect," he says, "intelligible objects are perceived by the intellect by means of the light which the First One spreads over them, and in seeing these objects, it sees really the intelligible light. But, as it gives its attention to the objects on which the light falls, it does not perceive with any exactness the principle which enlightens them, while if, on the contrary, it forgets the objects which it sees so as to contemplate only the brightness which makes them visible, it sees the light itself and the principle of the light. But it is never outside of itself that the intellect can contemplate the intelligible light. It then resembles the eye which, without contemplating an exterior or alien light, and indeed before it has even perceived it, is suddenly struck by a brightness which belongs to itself, or by a ray which darts from itself, and appears to it in the midst of darkness: it is just the same when the eye, so as to see no other objects, closes its lids and draws its light from itself, or when, pressed by the hand, it perceives the light which it has in itself. Then, although seeing no outside thing, it still sees; it sees even more than at any other time, for it sees the light. The other objects which it saw before, although they were luminous, were not the light itself. So, when the intellect closes its eye in some degree to other objects, and concentrates it on itself, then, seeing nothing, it yet sees, not an alien light which shines in alien forms, but its own light, which all at once shines inwardly with a pure radiance."

Again he says: "The soul which studies God must form an idea of Him whom it seeks to know; being aware, moreover, to what greatness it desires to unite itself, and persuaded that it will find blessedness in that union, it must plunge into the depths of divinity, until, instead of contemplating itself, or the intelligible world, it becomes itself an object of contemplation, and shines with the brightness of conceptions which have their source above."

We have here almost all that human wisdom can tell us; almost all that the prince of transcendental metaphysicians could express; as for other explanations, we must find them in ourselves, in the depths where all explanation disappears in its expression. For it is not only in heaven and earth, but above all in ourselves, that there are more things than all philosophies can contain; and as soon as we are no longer obliged to formulate the mysteries within us, we are more profound than all that has been written, and greater than all that exists.

I have translated this book, then, solely because I believe that the writings of the mystics are the purest diamonds in the vast treasure of humanity. A translation may indeed very easily be useless, for experience seems to prove that it matters little whether the mystery of the incarnation of a thought takes place in darkness or in light; it is enough that it has taken place. But, however this may be, the truths of mysticism have a strange privilege over ordinary truths; they can neither grow old nor die. There is no truth which did not, one morning, come down upon this world, lovely in strength and in youth, and covered with the fresh and wondrous dew which lies on things yet unspoken: today you may pass through the infirmaries of the human soul, where all thoughts come day by day to die, and you will not find there a single mystic thought. They have the immunity of the angels of Swedenborg, who progress continually towards the spring of their youth, so that the oldest angels appear the youngest; and whether they come from India, from Greece, or from the North, they have neither country nor date, and wherever we meet them, they are calm and real as God Himself. A work grows old in exact proportion to its anti-mysticism; and that is why this book bears no date. I know that it is unusually obscure, but I believe that a sincere and honest author is never obscure in the eternal sense of the word, because he always understands himself, and in a way which is infinitely beyond anything that he says. It is only artificial ideas which spring up in real darkness, and flourish solely in literary epochs and in the insincerity of self-conscious ages, when the thought of the writer is poorer than his expression. In the former case, we have the rich shade of a forest; in the latter, the gloom of a cavern, in which only dismal parasites can grow. We must take into account that unknown world which our author's phrases were meant to enlighten through the poor double horn-panes of words and thoughts. Words, as it has been said, were invented for the ordinary uses of life, and they are unhappy, restless, and as bewildered as beggars round a throne, when, from time to time, some royal soul leads them elsewhere. And, from another point of view, is the thought ever the exact image of that unknown thing which gave it birth? Do we not always behold in it the shadow of a conflict like that of Jacob with the angel, confused in proportion to the stature of the soul and of the angel? "Woe to us," says Carlyle, "if we have nothing in us except that which we can express and show to others." I know that on these pages there lies the shadow cast from objects which we have no recollection of having seen. The monk does not stop to explain their use to us, and we shall recognise them only when we behold the objects themselves on the other side of this life; but meanwhile, he has made us look into the distance, and that is much. I know, besides, that many of his phrases float almost like transparent icicles on the colourless sea of silence, but still they exist; they have been separated from the waters, and that is sufficient. I am aware, finally, that the strange plants which he cultivated on the high peaks of the spirit are surrounded by clouds of their own, but these clouds annoy only gazers from below. Those who have the courage to climb see that they are the very atmosphere of these plants, the only atmosphere in which they can blossom in the shade of non-existence. For this is a vegetation so subtle that it can scarcely be distinguished from the silence from which it has drawn its juices and into which it seems ready to dissolve. This whole work, moreover, is like a magnifying glass turned upon darkness and silence; and sometimes we do not immediately discern the outline of the ideas which are still steeped therein. It is invisible things which appear from time to time, and some attention is obviously needed for their recognition. This book is not too far off from us; probably it is in the very centre of our humanity; it is we, on the contrary, who are too far from the book; and if it seems to us discouraging as the desert, if the desolation of divine love in it appears terrible, and the thirst on its summits unendurable, it is not that the book is too ancient, but that we ourselves are perhaps old and sad and lacking in courage, like gray-haired men in presence of a child. Plotinus, the great pagan mystic, is probably right when he says to those who complain that they see nothing on the heights of introspection: "We must first make the organ of vision analogous and similar to the object which it is to contemplate. The eye would never have perceived the sun, if it had not first taken the form of the sun; so likewise the soul could never see beauty if it did not first become beautiful itself; and all men should begin by making themselves beautiful and divine, in order that they may obtain the sight of the beautiful and of divinity."

---

1. I shall give only one example, which is elementary in both senses of the word. Ruysbroeck distinguishes three kinds of life—the active life, the inward life, and the super-essential life. The Gnostics distinguish the spirit, the soul, and the material life, and divide men into three classes—the pneumatic or spiritual men, psychic or soul men, and hylic or material men. Plotinus also distinguishes between the soul, the intellect, the reasonable soul, and the animal nature. The Zohar distinguishes the spirit, the soul, and the life of the senses, and in the two systems, as in Ruysbroeck, the relation of the three principles is explained by a *procession* which is of the nature of an *irradiation*; then the theory of the divine meeting, God coming into us from within towards without, we going to Him from without towards within, etc. Cf. also the 5th Ennead, etc. etc.

II

THE life of Jean von Ruysbroeck, like that of most of the great thinkers of this world, is entirely an inner life. He said himself, "I have no concerns outside." Nearly all his biographers, Surius among others, wrote nearly two centuries after his death, and their work seems much intermixed with legend. They show us a holy hermit, silent, ignorant, amazingly humble, amazingly good, who was in the habit of working miracles unawares. The trees beneath which he prayed were illumined by an aureole; the bells of a Dutch convent tolled without hands on the day of his death. His body, when exhumed five years after his soul had quitted it, was found in a state of perfect preservation, and from it rose wonderful perfumes, which cured the sick who were brought from neighbouring villages. A few lines will suffice to give the facts which are undoubtedly authentic. He was born in the year 1274 at Ruysbroeck, a little village between Hal and Brussels. He was first a priest in the church of Sainte-Gudule; then, by the advice of the hermit Lambert, he left the Brabant town and retired to Grönendal (Green Valley) in the forest of Soignes, in the neighbourhood of Brussels. Holy companions soon joined him there, and with them he founded the abbey of Grönendal, the ruins of which may be seen to this day. Attracted by the strange renown of his theosophy and his supernatural visions, pilgrims from Germany and Holland, among them the Dominican Jean Tauler and Gerhard Groot, came to this retreat to visit the humble old man, and went away filled with an admiration of which the memory still lingers in their writings. He died, according to the *Necrologium Monasterii Viridis Vallis*, on the 2nd of December 1381, and his contemporaries gave him the title of "*L'Admirable.*"

It was the century of the mystics and the period of the gloomy wars in Brabant and Flanders, of stormy nights of blood and prayers under the wild reigns of the three Johns, of battles extending into the very forest where the saints were kneeling. St. Bonaventura and St. Thomas Aquinas had just died, and Thomas à Kempis was about to study God in that mirror of the absolute which the inspired Fleming had left in the depths of the Green Valley; while, first Jehan de Bruges, and afterwards the Van Eycks, Roger van der Weyden, Hugues van der Goes, Thierry Bouts, and Hans Memlinck were to people with images the lonely *Word* of the hermit.

Here is a list of the writings of Ruysbroeck, the sum-

total of which is very large. The Book of the Twelve Beguines; The Mirror of Eternal Salvation; The Book of the Spiritual Tabernacle; The Sparkling Stone; The Book of Supreme Truth; The Book of the Seven Steps of Spiritual Love; The Book of the Seven Castles; The Book of the Kingdom of the Beloved; The Book of the Four Temptations; The Book of the Twelve Virtues; The Book of Christian Faith, and The Adornment of the Spiritual Marriage. There are besides seven letters, two hymns, and a prayer, to which Surius gave these titles, Epistolae septem utiles, Cantiones duæ admodum spirituales, and Oratio perbrevis sed pia valde, the original texts of which I have not been able to discover in any of the Flemish manuscripts.

Some years ago the greater number of these writings were edited with the utmost care by a society of Flemish bibliophiles—*De Maetschappij der Vlaemsche Bibliophilen*—and most of this translation has been made from the excellent text of that edition.

I shall not undertake to give here an analysis of these different works; such an analysis would be difficult, monotonous, and useless. All the books of our author treat exclusively of the same science: a theosophy peculiar to Ruysbroeck, the minute study of the introversion and introspection of the soul, the contemplation of God above all similitudes and likenesses, and the drama of the divine love on the uninhabitable peaks of the spirit. I shall therefore content myself with giving some characteristic extracts from each of these writings.

The Book of the Twelve Beguines, in the Latin translation of Surius, is entitled *De vera contemplatione, opus præclarum, variis divinis institutionibus, eo quo Spiritus Sanctus suggessit ordine descriptis, exuberans*. This title explains more exactly the nature of the work, but is not to be found in any of the early manuscripts. The truth is that Ruysbroeck, following the custom of his age, seldom gave a title to his writings, and the titles by which they are now known, as well as the marginal rubrics of the chapters, have apparently been interpolated by the copyists. In the edition of the *Maetschappij der Vlaemsche Bibliophilen* we find collected under the title, *Dat boec van den twaelf beghinen*, first of all that treatise on the contemplative life mentioned by Surius, next a kind of manual of symbolical astrology, and lastly some thoughts on the passion and death of our Lord Jesus Christ. The three works are marked off from each other with more or less distinctness, and Ruysbroeck evidently fixes the place where he forsakes the inner universe and descends to the visible firmament, when he says at the end of chapter xxxi., "And after this I leave the contemplative life, which is God Himself, and which He grants to those who have renounced self and have followed His Spirit to where, in eternal glory, He rejoices in Himself and in His chosen."

The first eight chapters of this book are written in singular and very beautiful verses, and across their images, on the dark background of essential love, as across the windows of a burning convent, there flicker continually bright spiritual flames, and also frozen sadnesses, not unlike those of Villon or of Verlaine.

Here are some of these verses:—

"Contemplation is a science without
    mode,
Above human reason remaining
    evermore;
Unto our reason can it not come down,
Neither above it can reason ever rise.
Its enlightened freedom is a noble
    mirror,
Wherein the eternal splendour of God
    doth shine.
This modeless freedom hath no manner
    of its own,
And before it all the works of reason
    pale;
This modeless freedom is not God
    Himself,
But it is the light by which we see Him.
Those who move in this freedom unre-
    strained
In the light of God,
See vast prospects stretching out within
    them.
This modeless freedom is more high
    than reason,
Yet not without reason;
All things beholdeth it without
    surprise—
Surprise is far beneath it

*The life of contemplation is without
  surprise:
It sees, but knows not what is seen,
Above all things is it, and neither this
  nor that."*

Afterwards, the poet, perceiving that his verses are becoming too obscure, standing as he is on the threshold of eternal knowledge, says suddenly and very simply—

*"Now must I cease from versing
And speak of contemplation clearly."*

From this point he makes use of a strange prose, dark as the fearful void into which he is gazing, resembling that fierce cold which reigns above all our images, with blue lights flashing over the black frosts of abstraction. And when he descends for a moment into the regions of similitudes, he touches only the most distant, the most subtle, and the most unknown; he loves, too, such things as mirrors, reflections, crystal, fountains, burning glasses, water-plants, precious stones, glowing iron, hunger, thirst, fire, fish, the stars, and everything that helps him to endow his ideas with visible forms—forms laid prostrate in the presence of love on these clear summits of the soul—and to give distinctness to those unheard-of truths which he calmly reveals. It is needless to say more, for you shall presently reach the threshold of that spiritual marriage, and from there behold the still tempest of joy, reaching as far as to the eternal heart of God. In one word, this man of all others went near to beholding thought as it will be after death, and showed a faint shadow of its rich growths of the future, in the midst of the incomprehensible effluence of the Holy Trinity. I believe that this is a work which we shall perhaps remember elsewhere and always. You shall see, too, that the most amazing outbursts of St. Teresa are hardly to be distinguished from the top of those unlighted, colourless, and airless glaciers to which we climb with him "beyond surprise and emotion, above reason and the virtues," in the dark symphony of contemplation.

I give a passage from the book: De altero veræ contemplationis modo:—

"After this comes another mode of contemplation.

"Those who have raised themselves into the absolute purity of their spirits by the love and reverence which they have for God, stand in His presence, with open and unveiled faces. And from the splendour of the Father a direct light shines on those spirits in which the thought is naked and free from similitudes, raised above the senses, above similitudes, above reason and without reason, in the lofty purity of the spirit.

"This light is not God, but is a mediator between the seeing thought and God. It is a light-ray from God or from the Spirit of the Father. In it God shows Himself immediately, not according to the distinction and the mode of His persons, but in the simplicity of His nature and His substance; and in it also the Spirit of the Father speaks in thought, lofty, naked, and without similitude, 'Behold me as I behold you.' At the same time the keenness of the pure eyes is revealed, when the direct brightness of the Father falls upon them, and they behold the splendour of the Father—that is to say, the substance or the nature of God in an immediate vision, above reason and without distinction.

"This brightness and this manifestation of God give to the contemplative spirit a real knowledge of the vision of God, as far as it can be enjoyed in this mortal state. In order that you may understand me clearly, I will give you an image from the senses. When you stand in the dazzling radiance of the sun, and turn away your eyes from all colour, from attending to and distinguishing all the various things which the sun illuminates, if then you simply follow with your eyes the brightness of the rays which flow from the sun, you shall be led into the sun's very essence; and so likewise, if you follow with a direct vision the dazzling rays which stream from the splendour of God, they will lead you to the source of your creation, and there you will find nothing else but God alone."

I come now to the second of the works enumerated above. *The Mirror of Eternal Salvation* (*Die Spieghel der Ewigher Salicheit*) is, like all the writings of the mystic, a study of the joys of introversion, or of the return of man into himself, until he comes into touch with God. It was sent by the admirable doctor and eminent contemplator of the Green Valley "To the dear Sister Margaret van Meerbeke, of the convent of the Clares at Brussels, in the year of our Lord 1359." In some manuscripts the work is entitled "Book of the

Sacraments," and it is indeed the poem of eucharistic love, above all distinctions and in the midst of the blinding effluence of God, where the soul seems to shake the pollen from its essence and to have an eternal foreknowledge. Here, as elsewhere, we would need, in order to realise even slightly these terrors of love, a language which has the intrinsic omnipotence of tongues which are almost immemorial. The Flemish dialect possesses this omnipotence, and it is possible that several of its words still contain images dating from the glacial epochs. Our author then had at his disposal one of the very oldest modes of speech, in which words are really lamps behind ideas, while with us ideas must give light to words. I am also disposed to believe that every language thinks always more than the man, even the man of genius, who employs it, and who is only its heart for the time being, and that this is the reason why an ignorant monk like this mysterious Ruysbroeck, was able, by gathering up his scanty forces in prayers so many centuries ago, to write works which hardly correspond to our senses in the present day. I translate from this book the following fragment:—

"See now, here must our reason and all definite actions give way; for our powers become simple in love, and are silent and bend low before the manifestation of the Father; for the manifestation of the Father raises the soul above reason, into nakedness without similitudes. There the soul is simple, pure, and emptied of everything, and in that pure emptiness the Father shows His divine brightness. Into that brightness there can enter neither reason nor the senses, observation nor distinction. All these things must remain underneath it, for that measureless brightness dazzles the eyes of the spirit, so that their lids must close under its inconceivable radiance. But the naked eye, above reason, and in the inmost depths of intelligence, is always open, and beholds and contemplates with naked vision that light by that light itself. There we have eye to eye, glass to glass, image to image. By these three things we are like unto God, and are united to Him. For this vision which strikes upon our naked eye is a living mirror which God has made in His image. His image is His divine brightness, and with it He has filled to overflowing the mirror of our soul, so that no other brightness and no other image can enter there. But this brightness is not an intermediary between God and us; for it is the thing which we see, and also the light by which we see, but not our eye which sees. For although the image of God is without intermediary in the mirror of our soul, and is united to Him, still the image is not the mirror, for God does not become the creature. But the union of the image with the mirror is so great and so noble that the soul is called the mirror of God.

"Further, that very image of God which we have received and which we carry in our souls is the Son of God, the eternal mirror of divine wisdom, in which we all dwell, and are continually reflected. Yet we are not the wisdom of God, otherwise we should have created ourselves, which is impossible and a suggestion savouring of heresy. For whatever we are and whatever we have, we have received all from God and not from ourselves. And although this sublimity is so great a thought for our soul, yet is it hidden from the sinner and from many righteous persons. And all that we can know by the light of nature is incomplete and savourless and without emotion, for we cannot contemplate God or find Him reigning in our souls without His aid and grace, and without diligently exercising ourselves in His love."

The Book of the Spiritual Tabernacle (*Dat boec van den Gheesteleken Tabernacule*). *In Tabernaculum Mosis et ad id pertinentia commentaria, ubi multa etiam Exodi, Levitici, Numerorum mysteria, divino spiritu explicantur*, as Surius describes it, is the longest work of the hermit, and contains a strange, naïve, and arbitrary interpretation of the symbols of the ark of the covenant, and of the sacrifices of the ancient law. I shall give somewhat copious extracts from this work, for it shows an interesting and brotherly aspect of his Flemish soul; and the artistic subtlety with which he labours to elucidate his emblems, as well as his amusing and childlike delight in certain effects of colour and of figures, reminds us now and then of his marvellous contemporaries of the Cologne school, the old dreamy painters, Meister Wilhelm and Lochner, and of the splendid succession of nameless dreamers, who, in lands far off from his, gave a fixed form to the almost supernatural reflections of the spiritual joys of that and the following century, which passed away so near to God and so far from earth.

Here is what he says with regard to the offering of the poor as commanded in the Jewish law:—

"And they (the doves) shall keep near streams and

beside clear waters, so that if any bird flies downwards to seize them or to do them any injury, they may recognise him by his reflection in the water and beware of him. The clear water is Holy Scripture, the lives of saints, and the mercy of God. We shall reflect ourselves therein when we are tempted, and so none shall be able to hurt us. These doves have a loving nature, and young doves are often born of them, for whenever, to the glory of God and for our own felicity, we think of sin with scorn and hatred, and of virtue with love, we give birth to young doves—that is to say, to new virtues."

In the following passages he pictures, with the help of these same doves, the offering of Saint Paul:—

"And our Lord replied that His grace should be sufficient for him, for virtue is perfected in the weakness of temptations. When he understood this he offered these two doves into the hands of our Lord. For he renounced self, and willingly became poor, and bent the necks of his doves (that is, his desires) under the hands of our Lord Jesus Christ and of the Holy Church. And Christ broke the necks and the wings of the doves, and then he became incapable of desiring or of flying towards any desire except that which was God's will. And then Christ placed the head (that is to say, the will, which was dead and powerless) under the broken wings, and then the doves were ready to be consumed; and so the holy apostle says: 'Most gladly, therefore, will I rather glory in my weakness, that the power of Christ may rest upon me.'"

Let us consider further the extraordinary interpretation of the spiritual flowers embroidered on the hangings of the tabernacle:—

"On these four curtains of divers colours the Lord ordered Bezaleel and Aholiab to weave and to embroider with the needle many ornaments. So likewise our obedient will and our intelligence will place upon these four colours divers ornaments of virtues. On the white colour of innocence we shall place red roses, by evermore resisting all that is evil. Thus we maintain purity and crucify our own nature, and these red roses with their sweet perfume are very lovely on the white colour. Again, upon innocence we shall embroider sunflowers, by which we mean obedience; for when the sun rises in the east, the sunflower opens towards its rays, and turns ever eagerly towards the sun, even until its setting in the west; and at night it closes and hides its colours and awaits the return of the sun. Even so will we open our hearts by obedience towards the illumination of the grace of God, and humbly and eagerly will we follow that grace so long as we feel the warmth of love. And when the light of grace ceases to awaken fresh emotions, and we feel the warmth of love but little, or feel it not at all, then it is night, when we shall close our heart to all that may tempt it; and so shall we shut up within ourselves the golden colour of love, awaiting a new dawn, with its new brightness and its fresh emotions; and thus shall we preserve innocence always in its pristine splendour. On the blue colour, which is like the firmament, we shall embroider birds with varied plumage; in other words, we shall keep before our minds, with clear observation, the lives and the works of the saints, which are manifold. These works are their varied plumage, so gracious and so beautiful, and with this they adorned themselves and soared to heaven. They are birds which we must observe with attention; if we are like them in their plumage, we shall follow them to their eternal rest. On the purple colour (that is, violet or blood-red, meaning generosity) we shall place water-lilies, and these symbolise the free possession of all the treasures of God. For we notice four things in the water-lily. It keeps itself always above the water, and has four green leaves between the air and the water; and it is rooted in the earth, and above it is opened out to the sun; and it is a remedy for those who are fevered. So also may we, by generosity and freedom of spirit, possess the waves of all the riches of God. And between this free possession by our spirit and the waves of the lavish gifts of God, we shall have green leaves—that is to say, an earnest consideration of the way in which the eternal liberality of God flows forth, with ever new gifts to men, and we shall consider also how the gifts are bestowed with discrimination, according to the nature of the beloved ones who receive them, and how the final cause of all the gifts is the generous outflow of divine love; and the more immediate cause the wisdom and generosity in human creatures, which makes them resemble God. For none can know the wealth of the gifts of God except the wise and generous man, who, out of the treasures of God, can give wisely and generously to all creatures. So shall we adorn generosity, and then we shall be rooted in the soil of all the gifts—that is to say, in the Holy Spirit, as the water-lily is rooted deep down under the water. And we shall open our hearts in the air above, towards truth and towards the sun of righteousness. And thus we are a remedy for all the world; for the generous heart which possesses the treasures of God, ought to fill, console, refresh, and cool all those who are afflicted. And it is thus that the purple colour is adorned with the red colour—that is to say, with burning love. On it we shall place bright stars, by which I mean pious and devout prayer for the good of our neighbour, and reverent and secret communion between God and ourselves. These are the stars which illuminate with their brightness the kingdoms of heaven and of earth, and they make us inwardly light-giving and fruit-bearing, and fix us in the firmament of eternal life."

I shall next translate the whole of the "chapter on fishes," with its amazing analogies:—

"This is why the symbolic law ordered the Jews to eat clean fish, which had scales and fins; and all other fish were unclean and were forbidden by the law. By this we understand that our inner life ought to have a clothing of virtues, and our inward devotions ought to be covered with the application of our reason, just as the fish is clothed and adorned with its scales. And our loving power should move in four different ways:—in triumphing over our own will, in loving God, in desiring to resist our own nature, and in seeking to acquire virtues. These are four fins between which our inward life should swim, as fish do, in the water of divine grace. The fish has besides, in the middle of its body, a straight fin, which remains motionless in all its movements. So our inward feelings, firmly centred, should be empty of everything and without personal preference; in other words, we should allow God to act in us and in all things, both in heaven and earth. The fourth scale balances us in the mercy of God and in true divine peace. And so our devotion has fins and scales and becomes for us a pure nourishment which pleases God. But the scales which clothe and adorn our inward exercises should be of four colours, for some fish have gray scales, others red scales, others green scales, and others again white scales. The gray scales teach us that the images with which we clothe our devotions must be humble; in other words, we must think of our sins, of our want of virtue, of the humility of our Lord Jesus Christ, and of His mother, and of all things which may abase and humble us, and we shall love poverty and contempt and to be unknown and despised by everybody. This is the gray colour, which is very beautiful in the eyes of God.

"Further, we shall clothe our devotions with red scales—that is to say, we shall remember that the Son of God laid down His life for love of us, and we shall keep His passion in our memory, like a glorious mirror before our inward eyes, so that we may remember His love and console ourselves in all our sorrows. And we shall also think of the many torments of the martyrs, who by their sufferings followed our Lord into eternal life. These are red scales, set well in order, and they are a delightful clothing for our inward emotions.

"Then, again, we shall adorn our secret thoughts

with green scales. I mean that we shall earnestly meditate upon the noble lives of confessors and saints, remembering how they despised the world, and by what wonderful work and in what divers ways they honoured and served God. Green is the colour which attracts and rejoices loving hearts and willing eyes. Let us stir our fins, then, and follow the saints by imitating their good works to the utmost of our power.

"Again, we shall clothe our inward exercise with white scales; in other words, we shall glass ourselves in the purity of virgins, and shall observe how they fought and how they conquered flesh and blood, by which is meant the inclination of nature. This is why they wear the crown of gold and follow the Lamb, who is Christ, with new songs, which none shall sing save those who have preserved chastity in soul and body. But if we have lost purity, we may still acquire innocence and clothe ourselves with other virtues, and so we may reach the day of judgment shining brighter than the sun, and possess the glory of God through an unending eternity. In this way, then, we shall cover our inward devotion with four kinds of scales, and each kind shall have the active fins of good-will; that is, we must desire to carry out in good works that which we understand by our intelligence. So shall our spiritual nourishment be clean; for knowledge and wisdom without a virtuous life are like scales without fins; and practical virtues without reflection are fins without scales; and so we must know, love, and practise virtues, in order that our life may be pure; and then we shall be nourished with clean fish which have scales and fins."

I give next the following passage:—

"Further, each lamp had a vase of gold, full of water, in which was extinguished the fire taken away from the wicks. By this we learn that every gift demands from our mind a desire towards every cardinal virtue—a desire so simple that we can feel in ourselves the yearning of love after union with God. We observe this in Jesus Christ, who is our mirror in all things; for in every virtue which He practised, He excelled so lovingly that He sought ardently after union with His Father. And we shall unite all our yearnings in that loving yearning which He felt towards His Father in all cardinal virtues. For our loving yearnings are our golden vases, full of water—that is, of truth and righteousness—we shall plunge into them our burning wicks, the acts, that is, of all the virtues which we have practised; we shall plunge them in and extinguish them, by commending ourselves to His righteousness, and by uniting ourselves to His adorable merits; without this the wick of all our virtues would smoke and would have an evil savour before God and before all His saints."

Elsewhere, he examines the twelve jewels of the Breastplate, and sees in them reflections of eternal symbols, as well as unsuspected, precise, and suggestive analogies. Let us see whether it is not so.

"In the rays of the sun, the topaz surpasses in splendour all precious stones; and even so does the humanity of our Lord Jesus Christ excel in glory and in majesty all the saints and all the angels because of His union with the eternal Father. And in this union the reflection of the Divine Sun is so clear and glorious that it attracts and reflects in its clearness all the eyes of saints and angels in immediate vision, and those also of just men to whom its splendour is revealed. So likewise does the topaz attract and reflect in itself the eyes of those who behold it, because of its great clearness. But if you were to cut the topaz it would darken, while if you leave it in its natural state it will remain clear. And so, too, if you examine and try to penetrate the splendour of the eternal Word, that splendour will darken and you will lose it. But leave it as it is, and follow it with earnest gaze, and with self-abnegation, and it will give you light."

Let us next consider the curious correspondences which he discovered in other precious stones:—

"In this article we compare Christ to the noble sapphire, of which there are two kinds. The first is yellow with shades of purple and seems to be mingled with powdered gold; the other is sky-blue, and in the rays of the sun it gives forth a burning splendour, and one cannot see through it. And we find all this in our Lord, in this fifth article of the creed. For when His noble soul rose to heaven, His body lay in the tomb—yellow, because of the soul's departure; purple, because of His bleeding wounds; and mingled with powdered gold because He was united to the divine nature. And His soul descended into hell, blue as the sky, so that all his friends rejoiced and were glad in His splendour; and in His resurrection the splendour becomes so great and so powerful, both in body and soul, through the illumination of the Divine Sun, that it darts forth lightnings and burning rays, and inflames with love all things which it touches. And none can see through that noble sapphire, Christ, because in His divine nature there is a depth unfathomable."

I pass over the amethyst "from which red roses seem to flow forth," and as a closing passage from this work, I shall translate the last three symbols: those of the chrysolite, the emerald, and the jasper.

First of all, the chrysolite:—

"The communion of saints and the forgiveness of sins are obtained by the *waves of the night*—that is to say, by two sacraments of the Holy Church, baptism and penance. These are the waves which by faith wash that night of darkness, sin. And God has sworn, even from the time of Abraham, that He would give Himself to us and would become our familiar friend, and because of His all-embracing and overflowing love, He has willed to wash us in His blood. And in order that we might believe without doubting in the oath which He sware by Himself, He has sealed it with His own death, and has given the merits of His death to all men in the Holy Church for the remission of sins, and to the saints, for the adornment of their glory. That precious stone, the chrysolite, symbolises to us that article of the creed, 'the communion of saints, the forgiveness of sins,' for it is like the waves of the sea, translucent and green, and moreover it has gleams of gold. And so likewise all saints and just men are translucent by grace or by glory, and they are green by their holy life, and they gleam with the gold of divine love which shines through them. And these three adornments are common to all saints and to all just persons, for they are the treasure of the holy churches, here and in eternal life. And all who by penance have put away from them the colour of the Red Sea—that is, a sinful life—are like the chrysolite.

"You must know that this sea is red because of its country and the colour of its bed. It is between Jericho and Zoar, Jericho signifies 'the moon,' and Zoar the beast which blinds the reason. Between the moon of inconstancy and the inclination of reason towards the beast, there is always the Red Sea—that is to say, an impure life. No creature can live in the Red Sea, and whatever does not live in it sinks to the bottom; and that is why it is called the Dead Sea, because there is no movement in it, and it is like bitumen or pitch, because it seizes and slays whatever enters it, and in this way it very closely resembles sin, which seizes man and puts him to spiritual death in the sight of God, and plunges him into hell."

Let us see, lastly, how he applies the emerald and the jasper to the third and sixth articles of the Apostles' Creed:—

"In this article we compare to the Son of God that beautiful stone which is called the emerald, and which is so green that neither leaves nor grass nor any other green thing can compare with its viridity. And it fills and feeds with its greenness the eyes of those who behold it. Now when the eternal Word of the Father was made man, then was seen the greenest colour ever known on earth. That union of natures is so green and so lovely and so joyful, that no other colour can equal it; and so in a holy vision it has filled and fed the eyes of such men as have prepared themselves to perceive it. Nothing is more lovely and more pleasant to the eye than the emerald when it has been cut and polished, and everything that it reflects may be recognised and seen as in a mirror. And so, if we examine in detail the divine being of Him who took our nature through His love for us, we must needs admire, and we cannot sufficiently praise its sublimity. And when we consider how He became man, we must be ashamed of ourselves, remembering His humility, and we cannot abase ourselves too deeply. And when we remember what His motive was in becoming man, we cannot rejoice enough or love Him as He deserves.

"In these three ways we shall behold with eager desire, and we shall polish and lovingly examine Christ our noble emerald; and so doing, we shall find nothing more pleasant to the eyes of our reason, nothing more attractive, for we shall find Him reflected in us, and we shall find ourselves re-echoed in Him through His grace and a virtuous life, and so we shall turn away from earthly things and keep this mirror ever before our eyes.

"In another article we compare Christ to the noble jasper, which has a green colour, very pleasant to the eye; and it almost equals the emerald in its greenness. And so we compare it to the ascension of our Lord, who was green and beautiful in the eyes of the apostles, and so pleasant that they could never forget Him during all their lives. And we shall rightly have the same experience; we shall consider that the noble emerald, the eternal Word, descended into our nature because of His love for us, with an overflowing greenness, and we shall rejoice in this above all, for this vision is full of grace. We shall further consider that the glorious jasper, by which I mean our Lord Jesus, ascended to heaven wearing our nature, and is seated at the right hand of the Father, and has prepared for us the state of glory—Amen."

Next comes *The Book of the Twelve Virtues*, which Laurentius Surius entitles more exactly *Tractatus de præcipuis quibusdam virtutibus*. In it the hermit of Grönendal seems to have made a violent effort to open his bodily eyes, and all his thoughts are intertwined with the simplicity of divine children, in the green and blue rays of humility and mercy, while his prose, which is usually quite impersonal, is enlivened here with various counsels and practical matters.

Here is a fragment on humility:—

"To reach the lowest place is to have no longer any desire towards evil; and as we have always some sin to forsake, so long as we are in this mortal life, we never reach the lowest place, for to die is to attain, not according to the senses, but in a spiritual paradox. And if any one were to say that to be steeped in humility is to have reached the lowest place, I should not contradict his opinion. But it seems to me that to bathe oneself in humility is to bathe oneself in God, for God is the source of humility, and He is at the same height and the same depth above and below all places. And between self-abasement and the attainment of the lowest place, there is, to my mind, a difference. For to reach the lowest place is to have no longer any desire towards evil, and to experience self-abasement is to be steeped in humility, and that is self-annihilation in God and death in God. Now, we have always something to forsake so long as we live, and to have nothing more to forsake is to have reached the lowest place. This is why we cannot attain to the lowest place. For what man was ever so humble that he could not have been more humble still? and who ever loved so fervently that he could not have loved more fervently still? Except Christ, assuredly not one. And so let us never be satisfied while in this dying life, for we may always become more humble than we are to-day. It is a most joyful thought that we have so great and good a God that we can never give Him sufficient homage and praise. Yes, not even if each single man could give every moment that which is given by all men and by all angels. But if we steep ourselves in humility, that is enough, and we please God by Himself, for in that immersion we are *one life* in Him, not according to nature, but by being bathed in humility, because by humility we have descended below our creation, and we have flowed into God, who is the source of humility. And there we lack nothing, for we are beyond ourselves and in God, and there is neither giving nor receiving, nor anything which can be called *there*, for it is neither *there* nor *here*, but I know not where."

From the same book I transcribe the following passage on detachment from all things:—

"Now, he who has found God thus reigning in him by His grace, and who dwells in God above the measure of his human strength, may remain insensible to joy, to grief, and to the multitude of creatures. For God is *essenced* in him, and he is more disposed to introversion than to extroversion; and this essence is recalled to him wherever man is found; and this inclination and this essence are never forgotten, unless the man should deliberately turn away from God; and this he will not readily do, for he who has experienced God in this way cannot easily turn away from Him. I do not say that this can never happen, for no one is certain of anything in this mortal life, except of certain revelations.

"God takes by His divine power the man whom he has *essenced* in himself in this way, and enlightens him in everything, for everything is full to him of divine enjoyment; for he who refers all things to the glory of God, enjoys God in all things, and he sees in them the image of God. For he takes all from the hand of God, thanks Him and praises Him in everything, and God shines ever brightly before him, for he watches God with close attention, and never willingly turns away to worthless things. And as soon as he sees that he has turned towards worthless things, he at once turns away from them with great bitterness against himself, and bewails his unfaithfulness to God and resolves never again to turn knowingly towards worthless things. For all is bare and empty in which there is not either the glory of God or the good of our neighbour or our own salvation. He who thus watches over himself is less and less distracted, for his friend is often present with him, and that delights him above all. He is like to one who has a burning thirst. In his thirst he does nothing but drink. He may think of many other things besides the thirst which consumes him; but whatever he does, and whoever he is, or of whatever object he thinks, the image of drink does not disappear from his mind so long as he suffers from thirst. And the longer the thirst endures, the greater is the suffering of the man. And it is even so with the man who loves anything so passionately that he has no taste for aught besides, while nothing really touches his heart except that with which he is busied, and on which his love is set. Wherever he may be, with whomsoever he may find himself, nothing removes from him that which he so ardently loves. And he sees in all things the image of the beloved object; and the greater and more powerful his love, the more vividly that image is present to him. He does not seek repose and idleness that he may enjoy it, for no distraction hinders him from having the image of the beloved abiding ever with him."

Let us glance next at the little work on *Christian Faith*, to which Surius gives the title *De fide et judicio, tractatulus insignis*. Its twenty pages form a kind of catechism, splendid in its precision, from which I take the following fragment on the happiness of the elect:—

"We shall behold with our inward eyes the mirror of the wisdom of God, in which shall shine and be illumined all things which have ever existed and which can rejoice our hearts. And we shall hear with our outward ears the melody and the sweet songs of saints and angels, who shall praise God throughout eternity. And with our inner ears we shall hear the inborn Word of the Father; and in this Word we shall receive all knowledge and all truth. And the sublime fragrance of the Holy Spirit shall pass before us, sweeter than all balms and precious herbs that ever were; and this fragrance shall draw us out of ourselves, towards the eternal love of God, and we shall taste His everlasting goodness, sweeter than all honey, and it shall feed us, and enter into our soul and our body; and we shall be ever an hungered and athirst for it, and because of our hunger and thirst, these delights and this nourishment shall remain with us for ever, ever more renewed; and this is eternal life.

"We shall understand by love and we shall be understood by love, and God shall possess us and we Him in unity. We shall enjoy God, and, united to Him, we shall rest in blessedness. And this measureless delight, in that super-essential rest, is the ultimate source of blessedness, for we are then swallowed up in satisfaction beyond all possibility of hunger. Hunger can have no place in it, for there is nothing here but unity; all loving spirits shall here fall asleep in super-essential darkness, and nevertheless they shall live and wake for ever in the light of glory."

Next we come to *The Book of the Sparkling Stone, De Calculo, sive de perfectione filiorum Dei, libellus admirabilis,* as Surius adds. Here the subject is the mysterious stone of which the Spirit says in the Apocalypse: *Et dabo illi (vincenti) calculum candidum, et in calculo nomen novum scriptum, quod nemo scit nisi qui accepit* (Rev. ii. 17). This stone, according to the monk of the forest of Soignes, is the symbol of Christ, given to His loved ones only, and like a flame which images the love of the eternal Word. And then again we have glimpses of those dark shadows of love, from which break forth uninterrupted sobs of light, seen in awful flowers through the gradual expansions of contemplation and above the strange verdure of an unequalled gladness. Let us examine this passage:—

"And hence follows the third point, that is to say, an inward exercise above reason and without restraint; for that union with God which every loving spirit has possessed in love continually attracts and draws towards the inmost centre of its essence the divine persons and all loving spirits; and all those who love feel this attraction, more or less, according to their love and their holy exercises. And he who keeps guard over this attraction and clings closely to it cannot fall into deadly sin. But the contemplative one, who has renounced his own being and all things else, does not experience an expulsive force, because he no longer possesses anything, but is emptied of all; and so he can always enter naked and imageless into the secret place of his spirit. There he sees the eternal light revealed, and in that light he feels an eternal craving for union with God. And he himself feels a constant fire of love which desires above all things to be one with God. And the more he observes that attraction and that craving, the more keenly he feels it; and the more he feels it, the more he desires to be one with God, for he longs to pay the debt which God calls on him to pay. This eternal craving for union with God causes the spirit to glow evermore with love; but as the spirit uninterruptedly continues paying its debt, a perpetual consumption goes on within it; for in the refreshment of unity all spirits grow weary in their task, and feel only the absorption of everything into simple unity with God. This simple unity can be felt and possessed by none save by those who stand before the immense brightness and before love, above reason and without restraint. In this presence the spirit feels itself perpetually inflamed with love; and in this glow of love it finds neither beginning nor end. And it feels itself *one* with that burning fire of love. The spirit remains always on fire in itself, for its love is eternal, and it feels itself always consumed away in love; for it is attracted towards the refreshment of union with God, in which the spirit burns with love. If it observes itself, it finds a distinction and a difference between itself and God, but where it burns it is pure and has no distinction, and that is why it feels nothing else but unity; for the immeasurable flame of the divine love consumes and swallows up all that it has enveloped in its essence.

"And you may thus understand that the attracting unity of God is nothing else save boundless love, which lovingly draws inwards, in eternal enjoyment, the Father, the Son, and all who live in love. And we desire to burn and be consumed in that love everlastingly, for in it the blessedness of all spirits is found. And so we ought all to found our lives on a fathomless abyss; we shall thus be able to descend evermore in love, and to plunge ourselves beyond ourselves into its unsounded depths; and by the same love we shall rise and go beyond ourselves into its inconceivable height, and we shall wander in that measureless love, and it will lead us away into the boundless expanse of the love of God. And there will be a flow and outflow beyond ourselves, in the unknown pleasure of the divine goodness and riches. There will be an eternal fusion and transfusion, absorption and perabsorption of ourselves in the glory of God. See how, in each of these comparisons, I have shown to the contemplative mind its essence and its inward exercises. But no other can understand me, for no man can teach contemplation to his fellow. But when the eternal truth is revealed to the spirit, it is instructed in all that is needful."

I ought in fairness to translate also the many strange things in chapters vi., vii., and viii., which deal with "The difference between the hirelings and the faithful servants of God," "The difference between the faithful servants and the secret friends of God," and "The difference between the secret friends and the hidden sons of God." Here it does really seem as if the anchorite of the Green Valley had dipped into things beyond this world. But having run to such lengths already, I can hardly attempt it I must, however, be permitted to give the following fragment, which shall be the last from this book. It is strangely beautiful:—

"Understand, now, that this is the mode of progress: in our going towards God, we ought to carry our being and all our works before us, as an eternal offering to God; and in presence of God we shall surrender ourselves and all our works, and, dying in love, we shall pass beyond all creation into the super-essential kingdom of God. There we shall possess God in an eternal death to ourselves. And this is why the Spirit of God says in the book of the Apocalypse, 'Blessed are the dead who die in the Lord.' Rightly indeed does He call them the blessed dead, for they remain continually dead to themselves and immersed beyond their own nature in the gladdening unity of God. And they die ever newly in love, by the attracting refreshment of that same unity. Furthermore, the divine Spirit saith, 'They shall rest from their labours, and their works shall follow them.' In this finite existence, where we are born of God into a spiritual and virtuous life, we carry our works before us as an offering to God; but in that unconditioned life, where we die anew in God, into a life of everlasting blessedness, our good works follow us, for they are one life with us. In our walk towards God, God dwells within us; but in our death to ourselves and to all things besides, we dwell in God. If we have faith, hope, and love, we have received God, and He dwells in us with His mercies, and He sends us out as His faithful servants, to keep His commandments. And He calls us in as His mysterious friends, and we obey His counsels. But above all things, if we desire to enjoy God, or to experience eternal life within us, we must rise far above human reason, and enter into God through faith; and there we shall remain pure, at rest, and free from all similitudes, lifted by love into the open nakedness of thought. For when in love we die to all things, when in ignorance and obscurity we die to all the notice of the world, we are wrought and reformed by the eternal Word, who is an image of the Father. And in the repose of our spirit we receive the incomprehensible splendour which envelops and penetrates us, just as the air is penetrated by the brightness of the sun. And this splendour is merely a boundless vision and a boundless beholding. What we are, that we behold; and what we behold, that we are; for our thought, our life, and our essence are closely united with that truth which is God, and are raised along with it. And that is why in this pure vision we are one life and one spirit with God; and this is what I call a contemplative life. By connecting ourselves closely to God through love, we choose the better part; but when we thus behold God in super-essence, we possess Him altogether. This contemplation is united with an untrammelled inward devotion, that is to say, with a life in which earthly things are destroyed; for when we go outside ourselves into darkness and into unlimited freedom, the pure ray of the brightness of God shines perpetually on us; we are fixed in the ray, and it draws us out of ourselves into our super-essence till we are overwhelmed in love. And this overwhelming in love is always accompanied and followed by the free inward exercise of love. For love cannot be idle; it longs by knowledge and taste to enter into the immense riches which dwell in its inmost heart; and its hunger is inappeasable. To be always receiving in this powerlessness is to swim against the stream. We can neither leave nor take, do without nor receive, speak nor be silent, for it is above reason and intelligence, and higher than all created beings. And so we can neither attain nor pursue it; but we shall look within, and there we shall feel that the Spirit of God is leading us and drawing us on in this impatience of love. We shall look above, and there we shall feel that the Spirit of God is drawing us out of ourselves, and that we are lost in Him—that is, in the super-essential love with which we are one, and which we possess more deeply and more widely than all other things.

"This possession is a pure and profound enjoyment of all good and of eternal life; and we are swallowed up in this enjoyment, above reason and without reason, in the deep calm of Godhead, which shall nevermore be stirred. It is by experience only that we can know that this is true. For how this is, or who, or in what place, or what, neither reason nor inward exercise can tell us, and it is for this reason that our inward exercise which follows must remain without mode or limit. For we can neither conceive nor understand the unfathomable good which we possess and enjoy; neither by our inward exercises can we go out of ourselves to enter into it. And so we are poor in ourselves, but rich in God; hungry and thirsty in ourselves, satiated and full of wine in God; laborious in ourselves, in God enjoying perfect rest. And thus we shall remain throughout eternity. For without the exercises of love we can never possess God, and he who feels or thinks otherwise is deceived. And thus we live wholly in God, by possessing our beatitude, and we live wholly in ourselves by exercising our souls in love towards God; and although we live wholly in God and wholly in ourselves, yet it is but one life, which has two-fold and contrary sensations. For riches and poverty, hunger and satiety, work and idleness, these things are absolutely contrary to one another. Nevertheless, in this consists the nobility of our nature, now and everlastingly, for it is impossible that we should become God, or lose our created essence. But if we remain wholly in ourselves, separated from God, we shall be miserable and unsaved; and so we ought to feel ourselves living wholly in God and wholly in ourselves, and between these two sensations we shall find nothing but the grace of God and the exercises of our love. For from the height of our highest sensation, the splendour of God shines upon us, and it teaches us truth and impels us towards all virtues into the eternal love of God. Without interruption we follow this splendour on to the source from which it flows, and there we feel that our spirits are stripped of all things and bathed beyond thought of rising in the pure and infinite ocean of love. If we remained there continually, with a pure vision, we should never lose this experience, for our immersion in the enjoyment of God would be without interruption, if we had gone out of ourselves and were swallowed up in love, so possessing God. For if, overwhelmed in love, and lost to ourselves, we are the possessors of God, God is ours and we are His, and we plunge far beyond our depth, eternally and irrevocably having God as our own. This immersion in love becomes the habit of our being, and so it takes place while we sleep and while we wake, whether we know it or whether we know it not. And in this way it deserves no other praise; but it maintains us in possession of God and of all the good which we have received from His hands. It is like unto streams, which, without pause and without returning, flow continually into the sea, since that is the place to which they belong. And so, if we possess God alone, the immersion of our being through habitual love is always, and without return, flowing into an unfathomable emotion, which we possess, and which belongs to us. If we were always pure, and if we always beheld with the same directness of vision, we should have such a feeling as this. Now, this immersion in love is above all virtues, and above all the practices of love. For it is simply an eternal going forth out of ourselves, by a clear prevision, into a changed state, towards which we lean out of ourselves, as if towards our beatitude. For we feel ourselves eternally drawn outside ourselves and towards another. And this is the most secret and the most hidden distinction which we can experience between God and ourselves, and above it there is no more any difference. Nevertheless, our reason remains with its eyes open in the darkness—that is to say, in infinite ignorance—and in that darkness the boundless splendour remains secret and hidden from us, for the presence of its immensity blinds our reason. But it wraps us round with its purity and transforms us by its essence, and so we are wrought out of our personality and transformed until, overwhelmed in love, we possess our beatitude, and are one with God."

Let us next look at *The Book of the Seven Steps of the Ladder of Love* (called by Surius *De Septem Gradibus amoris, libellus optimus*) in which the prior of Grönendal studies seven virtues which lead from introversion to the confines of absorption. This seems to me one of the most beautiful works of a saint, whose works are all strange and beautiful I ought to translate from it some rather singular passages; among others, that in which he discusses the four melodies of heaven; but space fails us, and this introduction is already too long. I shall content myself with giving the following page:—

"The Holy Spirit cries in us with a loud voice and without words, 'Love the love which loves you everlastingly.' His crying is an inward contact with our spirit. This voice is more terrifying than the storm. The flashes which it darts forth open the sky to us and show us the light of eternal truth. The heat of its contact and of its love is so great that it well-nigh consumes us altogether. In its contact with our spirit it cries without interruption, 'Pay your debt; love the love which has loved you from all eternity.' Hence there arises a great inward impatience and also an unlimited resignation. For the more we love, the more we desire to love; and the more we pay of that which love demands, the greater becomes our debt to love. Love is not silent, but cries continually, 'Love thou love.' This conflict is unknown to alien senses. To love and to enjoy, that is to labour and to suffer. God lives in us by His grace. He teaches us, He counsels us, He commands us to love. We live in Him above all grace and above our own works, by suffering and enjoying. In us dwell love, knowledge, contemplation, and possession, and, above them, enjoyment. Our work is to love God; our enjoyment is to receive the embrace of love.

"Between love and enjoyment there is a distinction, even as between God and His grace. We are spirits when we hold fast by love, but when He robs us of our spirit, and re-makes us by His own spirit, then we are enjoyment. The Spirit of God breathes us out towards love and good works, and it breathes us in to rest and enjoyment; and that is eternal life, just as we breathe out the air which is in us and breathe in fresh air; and in that consists our mortal life and nature. And although our spirit should be ravished and its powers fail in enjoyment and in blessedness, it is always renewed in grace, in charity, and in virtues. And so what I love is to enter into a restful enjoyment, to go forth in good works, and to remain always united to the Spirit of God. Just as we open the eyes of the body, see, and shut them again, so quickly that we hardly notice what we have done, even so we die in God, we live out of God, and we remain always one with Him."

Next we have *The Book of the Seven Castles*, called by Laurentius Surius *De Septem Custodiis, Opusculum longe piissimum*. It is not without resemblance to the *Castle of the Soul*, by Saint Teresa of Avila, which has also seven dwellings, of which prayer is the door. The hermit of the forest of Soignes sends this work, with the *Mirror of Eternal Salvation*, "To the holy Clare, Margaret van Meerbeke, of the convent of Brussels," and so the counsels on which he touches in the prologue have a slight note of pitying sadness. For instance, he teaches her in what way she shall go to the window of the convent parlour, shutting out from her eyes the face of man; and speaks of the joy of pain and the care of the sick, with pale counsels for the sickward. Then there rise the seven spiritual castles of St.

Clara, the doors of which are closed by divine grace, and must no more be opened to look into the streets of the heart. Let us hear what follows, still on the subject of love:—

"And the loving soul cannot give itself wholly to God, nor perfectly receive God, for all that it receives is but a little thing as compared with that which it lacks, and counts as nothing in its eager emotion. And so it is disturbed, and falls into impatience, and into the strong passion of love; for it can neither do without God nor have Him, reach His depth nor His height, follow nor forsake Him. And this is the storm and the spiritual plague of which I have spoken; for no tongue can describe the many storms and agitations which arise from the two sides of love. For love makes a man now hot, now cold; now bold, now timid; now joyous, now sorrowful; it brings him fear, hope, despair, tears, complaints, songs, praises, and such things without number. Such are the sufferings of those who live in the passion of love; and yet this is the most spiritual and the most useful life which man can live, each according to his own capacity. But where man's method fails and can reach no higher, then God's method begins; where man, by his sufferings, his love, and his unsatisfied desires, entwines himself with God and cannot be united to Him, then the Spirit of our Lord comes like a fierce fire which burns and consumes and swallows up all things in itself, so that the man forgets his inward exercises, and forgets himself and feels just as if he were one spirit and one love with God. Here our senses and all our powers are silent, and they are calmed and satisfied, for the fountain of divine goodness and wealth has flowed over everything, and each has received more than he can desire.

"Next comes the third method, which we attribute to our heavenly Father—that in which He empties the memory of forms and images, and lifts up our naked thought to the ultimate source, which is Himself. There man is fixed firmly at his beginning, which is God, and is united to Him. And there is given to him strength and freedom to work inwardly and outwardly by means of all the virtues. And he receives knowledge and understanding in all exercises which are according to reason. And he learns how to receive the inward working of God and the transformation of the divine methods, which are above reason, even as we have already said. And above all divine limits, he will understand by the same boundless intuition, the boundless essence of God, whose being is without limitation. For one cannot express it by words, nor by works, nor by methods, nor signs, nor similitudes, but it manifests itself spontaneously to the simple intuition of pure and naked thought.

"But we may place on the road signs and similitudes which prepare man for the sight of the Kingdom of God, and you shall imagine this essence like the glow of a boundless fire, in which everything is silently consumed—a red and motionless conflagration. And so it is with the calm of essential love, which is the enjoyment of God and of all the saints, above all limitations, and above all the works and all the practices of virtue. This love is a wave, boundless and calmed, of riches and joys, in which all the saints are swallowed up with God in an unlimited enjoyment. And this joy is wild and lonely like a wandering, for it has neither limit, nor road, nor path, nor rest, nor measure, nor end, nor beginning, nor anything which one can show or express by words. And this is the pure blessedness of all of us, this divine essence, and our super-essence, above reason and without reason. If we desire to experience it, our spirit must go forth into it, above our created essence, towards that eternal centre in which all our lines begin and end. And in this centre these lines lose their name and all distinction, and are united to this centre, and become that same unity which the centre itself is; and nevertheless in themselves they always remain as converging lines.

"See, then, how we shall thus always remain what we are in our created essence, and yet by the ascent of our spirit we shall continually pass into our super-essence. In it we shall be above ourselves, below ourselves, beyond our breadth, beyond our length, in an eternal wandering which has no return."

I shall say little of the small work entitled *Four Temptations*, which deals with the very subtle dangers which threaten the contemplative mind, the most formidable of them all being quietism. With the exception of certain discoveries in the unknown psychology of prayer, this work, which, as I have said, is very short, does not present any very exceptionally lofty summit to our souls.

The other little work, which is about the same length—that is to say, about twenty pages—is called

The Book of Supreme Truth, or, according to Surius, *Samuel*. He adds:—"Qui alias de alta contemplatione dicitur, verius autem apologice quorumdam sancti hujus viri dictorum sublimium inscribi possit." But this book is so marvellous that one would need to translate the whole. At present I shall make no extract from it, since we can no more divide it than we can divide that essence whose perpetual effusion is displayed in its unique and awful mirror.

I come, therefore, to *The Book of the Kingdom of Lovers*, the strangest and most abstract work of the sage of the Green Valley, in the midst of which the soul stretches itself, and is filled with terror in a spiritual void which is doubtless normal, and which for the mind that does not follow it is like some dark glass bell, in which there is neither air, nor image, nor anything that can be exactly conceived, except uninterrupted stars in the eternal spaces.

The work is founded on that verse in Wisdom, "Justum deduxit per vias rectas et ostendit illi regnum Dei," and includes the three virtues of theology and the seven gifts of the Holy Ghost I proceed at once to translate, and more fully than ever.

Let us look first at this passage on the deserts of being:—

"The soul of man being made of nothing, which God took from nowhere, man has followed this nothingness, which is nowhere, and he has gone out of his ego into wanderings, by immersion in the simple essence of God, as in his own ultimate source; and he has died in God. To die in God is to be blessed; and, for each one according to his own merits, it involves a great difference both in grace and glory. This blessedness is to understand God and to be understood by God, in the joyful unity of the divine persons, and to have flowed by this unity into the super-essence of God. Now this unity brings joy when we look inward, and bears fruit in our outward life, and so the fountain of unity flows; that is to say, the Father begets the Son, the eternal truth, who is the image of the Father, in which He sees Himself and all things. This image is the life and cause of all creatures, for in this image is everything, according to the divine mode of being; and by this image all things are perfectly made, and all things are wisely ruled upon that model; and according to this image everything is set apart for its own end, so far as it is possible for God to do so; for every creature has received the means of attaining blessedness. But the reasonable creature is not the image of the Father, according to the effluence of his created mode of being, for that effluence flows forth in as far as it is a creature, and that is why it enjoys and loves with measure in the light of grace or of glory. For no one possesses the divine nature actively according to the divine mode, except the divine persons themselves, since no creature can work according to an infinite mode, for if it worked thus it would be God and not a creature.

"By His own image God has made His creatures like unto Himself in their nature, and in those who have turned to Him, He has made the likeness even greater—higher than nature in the light of grace or of glory, each one according to the capacity which he has by the state of his soul or by his merits. Now all those who feel this inward contact, who have an enlightened reason and the eagerness of love, and to whom love's infinite freedom has been revealed, enter into joyful contemplation in the super-essence of God. Moreover, God is united to His essence in a joyful manner, and contemplates that very essence which He enjoys. According to the mode of the enjoyment, the divine light constantly fails in the infinite essence; but in contemplation and in a fixed and steady gaze the vision cannot be darkened, for we shall forever behold that which we enjoy. Those for whom the light constantly fails are those who rest in enjoyments, in the midst of those wild solitudes where God possesses Himself in perpetual joy; there the light grows dim in rest and in the infinitude of the sublime essence. There God is His own throne, and all those who possess God in grace and in glory in this degree are the thrones and the tabernacles of God, and they have died in God in an eternal rest.

"From this death there arises a super-essential life —that is to say, a life of contemplation—and here the gift of intelligence begins. For God, who without ceasing contemplates the very essence which He enjoys, and who grants the impatience of love to those whom He makes like unto Himself, gives also rest and enjoyment to those who are united with Him. But where there is union of being and complete immersion, there is no more giving or receiving. And because He grants an enlightened reason to those whom He makes like unto Himself, He also gives a boundless splendour to those who are united to Him. That boundless splendour is the image of the Father. We are created in this image, and we are capable of being united to it in a grandeur more lofty than thrones, if we only contemplate, above our own human weakness, the glorious face of the Father—in other words, the sublime nature of deity. Now this unfathomed splendour is a common gift to all spirits who rejoice in grace and in glory. It thus streams forth for all like the splendour of the sun, and yet those who receive it are not all equally enlightened. The sun shines more clearly through glass than through stone, more clearly through crystal than through glass, and each precious stone shines and shows its beauty and its power and its colour in the light of the sun. Even so is each man enlightened both in grace and in glory, according as he is capable of receiving so sublime a gift; but he who is most enlightened in grace yet has less than he who is least enlightened in glory. Nevertheless the light of glory is not an intermediary between the soul and this unlimited splendour, but our spiritual condition, our earthly state, and our inconstancy disturb us, and so we have to gain merits, which those who dwell in glory have no need to gain.

"This sublime splendour is the simple contemplation of the Father, and of all those who behold and rejoice, and look fixedly in one direction by means of an incomprehensible light, each one according as the light is bestowed upon him. For that measureless light shines ceaselessly into all our thoughts; but the man who lives here, in this earthly state, is often overwhelmed with images, so that he does not always actively and steadily behold the super-essence of God by means of this light. But in receiving this gift he virtually possesses it, and he can contemplate whenever he wills. Since the light by which we contemplate is unlimited, and that which we contemplate of an unfathomed depth, the one can never reach the other; but this fixed gaze of our contemplation remains eternally turned towards the infinite, in the joyful presence of the sublime Majesty, where the Father, by His eternal wisdom, gazes fixedly into the depths of His own infinite being."

A great part of this book on *The Kingdom of Lovers* is written in singular verses. The three-lined and breathlessly monotonous rhythm is rather like that of the *Stabat Mater*, only that the third line of every strophe reproduces the same rhyme throughout the entire work, and rests on an abstract idea from which the two preceding lines rise, like twin flowers of obscurity and restlessness. We can imagine this hollow music floating through the spiritual dreams of the maids of Memlinck, while their secret senses, their faces, and their little hands all unite in ecstasy; but unhappily a translation cannot reproduce its taste of darkness and of bread soaked in the night, nor catch the image of the tear-brightened gloom, of ice mingled with fire, of oppression without hope, which we feel throughout the work. I shall therefore translate only one of these dark poems, the subject of which is the "Gift of Intelligence."

"He who seeks that gift to light him
Must rise beyond his nature,
To the highest height of being.
Brightness without measure
There shall he perceive it
In primal purity.
Through his soul will flow
The light of heavenly truth,
And he in it shall vanish.
That universal radiance
Enlightens the pure-hearted
According to their merits.
Then can they behold
With gaze that knows no limit
The very face of joy.
For ever shall we gaze on
That which we there enjoy
And lose ourselves in vision.
Far off has gone the Lover;
We turn our eyes for ever
Towards the blessed vision.
Yet has he reached the goal
And the lover has the loved one
In the lonely realm of union.
So shall we thus remain
And ever strive to follow
To that wondrous depth divine."

I should have liked to translate many other passages from this remarkable volume; but I shall close with a translation of the chapter entitled "Of the gift of sweet-savoured wisdom":—

"The seventh divine gift is that of sweet-savoured wisdom. It is granted on the highest peak of introversion, and it penetrates the intelligence and the will according as they are turned towards the absolute. This savour is without source and without measure, and it flows from within outwards, and drinks in the body and the soul (in proportion to their respective capacity for its reception) even to the inmost sense—that is to say, even to a physical sensation. The other senses, like sight and hearing, take their pleasure outside, in the marvels which God has created for His own glory and for the needs of men. This incomprehensible savour, above the mind and in the vast breadth of the soul, is without measure, and it is the Holy Spirit, the incomprehensible love of God. In lower regions than the spirit, sensation is limited. But as its powers are inherent, they overwhelm everything. Now, the eternal Father has adorned the contemplative spirit with joy in unity, and with active and passive comprehension in which the self is lost, and the spirit thus becomes the throne and the rest of God; and the Son, the eternal Truth, has adorned the contemplative intelligence with His own brightness, so that it may behold the face of joy. And now the Holy Spirit desires to adorn the contemplative will, and the inherent unity of its powers, so that the soul may taste, know, and feel how great God is. This savour is so vast that the soul imagines that heaven, earth, and all that is in them must dissolve and sink in nothingness before its unbounded sweetness.

These delights are above and beneath, within and without, and have entirely enveloped and saturated the kingdom of the soul. Then the intellect beholds the pure source from which all these delights flow forth. This awakes the attention of the enlightened reason. It knows well, however, that it is incapable of knowing these unimaginable delights, for it observes by means of a created light, while this joy is entirely without measure. Therefore the reason fails in its attention; but the intellect, which is transformed by this illimitable splendour, beholds without ceasing the incomprehensible joy of beatitude."

It remains now to say a word about the different translations of Ruysbroeck's work. Twenty years ago, Ernest Hello, who, with Villiers de l'Isle Adam and Stéphane Mallarmé, is the greatest French mystic of our time, published a brief volume in which he collected under headings, chosen mostly as his fancy dictated, various passages of our author, translated from a Latin translation written in the sixteenth century by Laurentius Surius, a Carthusian monk of Cologne. This translation of Surius, noble and subtle in its Latinity, gives with strict and admirable care the sense of the original; but with its over-anxiety, its prolixity, and its weakness, it resembles, when we contrast with it the crude colours of the original Flemish, some distant image seen through sullied panes. When his author uses one word, Surius generally employs two or three, and even then, still dissatisfied, he very often paraphrases once more that which he has already translated in full. The hermit utters cries of love so passionate that they are sometimes almost like blasphemies; Surius is frightened as he reads them and sets down something different. There are times when the old hermit looks outside himself, and in speaking of God searches for images drawn from the garden, the kitchen, or from the stars. Surius does not always venture to follow these flights, and he tries to weaken the meaning or flatters himself that he is ennobling it.

"He escapes me like a truant,"

says one of the Flemish Beguines in speaking of Jesus, and others add:—

> *"Christ and I keep house together,*
> *He is mine, I His;*
> *Night and day His love outwears me;*
> *He my heart hath stolen;*
> *In His mouth He holds me,*
> *What care have I outside!"*

Elsewhere God says to man:—

> *"I will be thy nourishment,*
> *Thy host and thy cook.*
> *My flesh was well roasted*
> *On the cross for love of thee.*
> *Shalt eat and drink with Me."*

The translator is terrified and changes these astonishing flights into pale circumlocutions. The wild and simple air, the vast and savage love of the original work, most frequently disappear in a wise, correct, copious, and monotonous conventual phraseology; the fidelity to the meaning remaining all the while exact. It was fragments of this translation which Ernest Hello translated in his turn, or rather, he gathered together in chapters arranged by himself, phrases taken from different portions of the work, and disfigured by a double translation. He thus formed a kind of anthology, admirable in its way, almost entirely consecutive; but in which, in spite of careful searching, I have been unable to find more than three or four passages reproduced in their entirety.

As for the present translation, its one merit is its literal exactitude. I might perhaps have been able to make it, if not more elegant, at least more readable, and to improve the work a little from the point of view of theological and metaphysical terminology. But it seemed to me less dangerous and more loyal to confine myself to an almost blind word-for-word translation. I have also resisted the inevitable temptation to introduce unfaithful splendours, for the mind of the old monk is constantly touching upon strange beauties, which his discretion does not awake, and all his paths are peopled with lovely sleeping dreams, whose slumber his humility does not venture to disturb.

M. Maeterlinck.

Selected passages from "The Adornment of the Spiritual Marriage."

On the Kingdom of the Soul

He who desires to obtain and to preserve virtue will adorn, occupy, and arrange his soul like to a kingdom. Free will is the king of the soul. He is free by nature, and yet more free through divine mercy. He will be crowned with a crown named charity. This crown and this kingdom we shall receive from the Emperor, who is the Lord, the Ruler and the King of kings, and we shall possess, rule, and maintain this kingdom in His name. The sovereign, free will, shall dwell in the highest town of the kingdom—that is to say, in the strong desires of the soul. And he will be adorned with a robe of two parts. The right side of the robe shall be a virtue which is called strength, so that he may be strong and powerful to conquer every obstacle, and to dwell at last in heaven in the palace of the great Emperor, bending his crowned head with love and passionate self-surrender before the supreme and sovereign King. This is the fitting work of charity. Through it we receive the crown. Through it we adorn the crown, and through it we maintain and possess the kingdom through all eternity. The left side of the robe shall be a cardinal virtue, which is called moral strength. Through its aid shall free will, the king, put down all immorality and fulfil all virtue, and shall have the power to maintain his kingdom unto death.

This king shall choose councillors in his country, the wisest to be found in the land. These will be two divine virtues, knowledge and discretion, enlightened by the grace of God. They will dwell near the king, in a palace which is called the soul's strength of reason; but they will be clothed and adorned with a moral virtue which is called temperance, so that the king may always act or refrain from acting according to their counsels. By knowledge we shall purge the conscience from all its faults and adorn it with every virtue; and by discretion we shall give and take, do and leave undone, speak and be silent, fast and eat, listen and reply; and in all things we shall act according to knowledge and discretion, clothed with their moral virtue, which is called temperance or moderation.

This king, free will, shall also set up in his kingdom a judge, who shall be called justice, a divine virtue when it springs from love; and it is one of the highest moral virtues. This judge shall dwell in the conscience, in the centre of the kingdom, in the strongest passions. And he will be adorned with moral virtue, which is called prudence. For justice cannot be perfect. This judge, justice, shall travel through the kingdom with the power and the force of the king, accompanied by wisdom of counsel and by his own prudence. He will promote and dismiss, judge and condemn, kill and keep alive, mutilate, blind and restore sight, lift up and put down, organise, punish, and chastise every sin with perfect justice, and at last destroy all vices.

The people of this kingdom—that is all the pure of soul—shall be established on and in the fear of God; they shall be subject unto God in all virtues, each according to his own capacity. He who has thus occupied, adorned, and regulated the kingdom of his soul, has gone forth in love and virtue towards God, himself, and his neighbour.

Christ the Sun of the Soul

The sun shines in the east, in the centre of the world, on the mountains; it hastens summer in that region, and creates good fruits and potent wines, filling the earth with joy. The same sun shines in the west, at the ends of the earth; there the country is colder, and the power of its heat is less, yet nevertheless it produces a great many excellent fruits; but few wines are found there.

Those men who dwell in the west of their own being, remain in the outward senses, and by their good intentions, their virtues, and their outward practices, through God's grace, they produce abundant harvests and virtues in various ways, but they seldom taste the wine of inward joy and of spiritual consolation.

The man who will feel the shining of the Eternal Sun, which is Christ Himself, will have clear vision, and will dwell on the mountains of the east, concentrating all his energies and raising his heart towards God, free and careless as regards joy, sorrow, and all creatures. There Christ the Sun of Righteousness shines on the free and uplifted heart; and these are the mountains which I have in mind. Christ, the glorious sun and the divine brightness, shines and illumines and enkindles by His inward coming, and the power of His Spirit, the free heart and all the powers of the soul.

When summer draws near, and the sun rises higher in the heavens, it draws the moisture of the soil through the roots and the trunk of the trees, until it reaches the branches, and hence come foliage, flowers, and fruits. So likewise, when Christ, the Eternal Sun, rises in our hearts, so that the summer reigns over their adornment of virtues, He sends His light and His fire into our will, and draws the heart from the multitude of earthly things, and creates unity and close fellowship, and makes the heart to grow and become green through inward love, and to bear the flowers of loving devotion and the fruits of gratitude and affection, and preserves these fruits in the sorrow and humility we feel because of our impotence.

The Lesson from the Bee

Observe the wise bee and make it your model. It dwells in a community in the midst of its companions, and it goes forth, not during the storm, but when the weather is calm and still and the sun is shining; and it flies towards all the flowers on which it can find sweetness. It does not rest on any flower, neither in its beauty nor in its sweetness, but it draws from each calix honey and wax—that is to say, the sweetness and the substance of its brightness—and it bears them back to the community in which all the bees are assembled, so that the honey and wax may profitably bear fruit.

The opened heart on which Christ, the Eternal Sun, is shining, grows and flourishes under His rays, and flows with all its inner powers into joy and sweetnesses.

. . .

Now the wise man will act like the bee, and he will fly out in order to settle with care, intelligence, and prudence on all the gifts and on all the sweetness which he has experienced, and on all the good which God has done to him; and through the rays of the sun and his own inward observation he will experience a multitude of consolations and blessings. And he will not rest on any flower of all these gifts, but, laden with gratitude and praise, he will fly back again toward the home in which he longs to dwell and rest for evermore with God.

The Dew of Mid-day

Sometimes in these burning days there falls the honey-dew of some false sweetness, which soils the fruits or completely spoils them. It falls for the most part at noon, in bright sunshine, and its great drops can hardly be distinguished from rain. Even so there are some men who can be caught away from their outward senses by some brightness which is the gift of the enemy. And this brightness enwraps and envelops them, and at that moment they behold images, falsehoods, and many kinds of truths, and voices speak to them in different ways, and all this is seen and received with great joy. And here there fall at times the honey-drops of a false sweetness in which the man delights himself. He who values it highly receives a great quantity, and so the man is often injured, for if he holds for true such things as have no resemblance to truth, because they have been shown or taught him, he falls into error and the fruit of virtue is lost. But those who have climbed by the paths which I have pointed out above, although they may indeed be tempted by that spirit and by that brightness, will recognise them and receive no injury.

The Lesson from the Ant

I will give a brief parable to those who live in continual ebullitions of love, in order that they may endure this disposition nobly and becomingly, and may attain to a higher virtue.

There is a little insect which is called the ant; it is strong and wise, and very tenacious of life, and it lives with its fellows in warm and dry soils. The ant works during summer and collects food and grain for the winter, and it splits the grain so that it may not become rotten or spoiled, and may be eaten when there is nothing more to be found. And it does not make strange paths, but all follow the same path, and after waiting till the proper time they become able to fly.

So should these men do; they will be strong by waiting for the coming of Christ, wise against the appearance and the inspiration of the enemy. They will not choose death, but they will prefer God's glory alone and the winning of fresh virtues. They will dwell in the community of their heart and of their powers, and will follow the invitation and the constraint of divine unity. They will live in rich and warm soils, or, in other words, in the passionate heat of love, and in great impatience. And they will work during the summer of this life, and will gather in for eternity the fruits of virtue. These they will divide in two—one part means that they will always desire the supreme joy of eternity; the other, that by their reason they will always restrain themselves as much as possible, and wait the time that God has appointed for them, and so the fruit of virtue shall be preserved into eternity. They will not follow strange paths or curious methods, but through all storms they will follow the path of love, towards the place whither love shall guide them. And when the set time has come, and they have persevered in all the virtues, they shall be fit to behold God, and their wings shall bear them towards His mystery.

What shall the Forsaken do?

He shall humbly consider that he hath nothing of his own save his misery, and shall say with resignation and self-abandonment the same words which were spoken by holy Job: "The Lord gave, and the Lord hath taken away; blessed be the name of the Lord." And in all things he shall yield up his own will, saying and thinking in his heart, "Lord, I am as willing to be poor and without all those things of which Thou hast deprived me, as I should be ready to be rich, Lord, if Thy will were so, and if in that state I might further Thy glory. It is not my natural will which must be done, but Thy will and the will of my spirit. Lord, I am Thine, and I should be Thine as gladly in hell as in heaven, if in that way I could advance Thy glory. So then, O Lord, fulfil in me the good pleasure of Thy will." Out of all sufferings and all renunciations the man will draw for himself an inward joy; he will resign himself into the hands of God, and will rejoice to suffer in promoting God's glory. And if he perseveres in this course, he will enjoy secret pleasures never tasted before; for nothing so rejoices the lover of God as to feel that he belongs to his Beloved. And if he has truly risen to this height in the path of virtues, it is not necessary that he shall have passed through the different states which we have pointed out in previous chapters, for he feels in himself, in work, in humble obedience, and in patience and resignation, the source of every virtue. This method has therefore an everlasting certainty.

At this season the sun enters into the sign of Libra, for the day and night are equal, and light and darkness evenly balanced. Even so for the resigned soul Jesus Christ is in the sign of Libra; and whether He grants sweetness or bitterness, darkness or light, of whatever nature His gift may be, the man retains his balance, and all things are one to him, with the exception of sin, which has been driven out once for all. When all consolation has been withdrawn from these resigned ones, so that they believe they have lost all their virtues, and are forsaken of God and of every creature; then, if they know how to reap the various fruits, the corn and wine are ripe and ready.

The Setting of the Eternal Sun

When the time came for Christ to gather in and bear away to the eternal kingdom the fruits of all the virtues that ever were and ever shall be practised upon earth, then the Eternal Sun began to set; for He humbled Himself and gave up the life of His body into the hands of His enemies. And in His distress he was misunderstood and forsaken by His friends, and all consolation, from without and from within, was taken away from His human nature, and it was overwhelmed with misery and pain, with scorn and heaviness, and in it He paid all the debt that justice claimed for sin. He suffered these things with humble patience, and in this resignation He fulfilled the highest tasks of love, and so He received and redeemed our eternal heritage. Thus was adorned the lower part of His noble humanity, for in it He suffered this sorrow for our sins. And this is why He calls Himself the Saviour of the world; this is why He is now famous and glorified, exalted and seated at the right hand of His Father, where He reigns with power. And every creature on earth, in heaven, and in hell, bends continually the knee before His glorious name.

The Nature of God

We must consider and examine the sublime nature of God: how it is simplicity and purity; height that cannot be scaled and depth that cannot be sounded; breadth without understanding and length without end; awful silence and the savage wilderness; rest of all saints in the union and in the common joy which He shares with His saints throughout eternity.

The Divine Generosity

The incomprehensible wealth and sublimity and the universality of the gifts which flow forth from the divine nature awake wonder in the heart of man, and above all he marvels at the universal presence of God and of His works, a presence which is above everything, for he beholds the inconceivable essence, which is the common joy of God and of all the saints. And he sees that the Divine Persons send forth one common effluence in works, in grace, and in glory, in nature and above nature, in all states and in all times, in men and in the glorified saints, in heaven and on earth, in all reasonable creatures, and in those which are without reason or material, according to the merits, the needs, and the receptivity of each. And he sees the creation of the heaven and the earth, the sun and the moon, the four elements with all the creatures, and the course of the heavens, which is common to all. God, with all His gifts, is common to all, men and angels are a common gift, and the soul with all its faculties....

When man thus considers the wealth and the marvellous sublimity of the divine nature, and all the manifold gifts which He grants and offers to His creatures, amazement is stirred up in his spirit at the sight of so manifold a wealth and majesty; at the sight of the immense faithfulness of God to all His creatures. This causes a strange joy of spirit, and a boundless trust in God, and this inward joy surrounds and penetrates all the forces of the souls in the secret places of the spirit.

Christ the Lover of all Men

Consider how Christ gave Himself to all in perfect faithfulness. His secret and sublime prayer flowed forth towards His Father, and was for the common good of all who desire salvation. Jesus Christ was all things to all men in His love, in His teaching, in His reproaches, in His consolations and sweetness, in His generous gifts, in His gracious forgiveness. His soul and His body, His life, His death, and His service were and are for the common good of all. His sacrament and His gifts are for all. Christ received neither food, nor drink, nor anything that was needful for His body, without thinking of the common good of all those who shall be saved even until the last day.

Christ had nothing of His own, but all was held in common, body and soul, mother and disciples, tunic and cloak. He ate and drank for us, He lived and toiled for us. His toil and grief and misery were indeed His own, but the blessings and the good which flowed from them were the common possession of all. And the glory of His merits shall be the possession of all throughout eternity.

How Christ gave Himself to us in the Sacrament

There is a special benefit which Christ, in the Holy Church, has left to all the good: namely, that supper of the great feast of Passover, which He instituted when the time had come for Him to leave His sorrow and go to the Father, after He had eaten of the paschal lamb with His disciples and the ancient law had been fulfilled. At the end of the meal and of the feast, He wished to give them a special food, which He had long desired to give. In this way He would make an end of the ancient law and bring in the new, and so He took bread in His sacred hands and consecrated His sacred body and afterwards His blood, and gave them to all His disciples, and left them as a common gift to all just men, for their eternal benefit.

This gift and this special food rejoice and adorn all great festivals and all banquets in heaven and on earth. In this gift Christ gives Himself to us in three ways: He gives us His flesh and His blood and His bodily life, glorified and full of joys and sorrows; and He gives us His Spirit, with its supreme faculties, full of glory and of gifts, of truth and justifying power; and He gives us His personality, with the divine light which raises His Spirit and the spirits of all enlightened beings into the sublime unity and joy of God.

Christ desires that we shall remember Him whenever we consecrate, offer, and receive His body. Consider now in what way we shall remember Him. We shall observe and examine how Christ inclines Himself towards us, by loving affection, by great desires, by a tender joy and warm influence passing into our bodily nature. For He gives us that which He received from our humanity, His flesh, His blood, and His bodily nature. We shall likewise observe and examine that precious body, tortured, furrowed, and wounded with love, because of His faithfulness towards us. So shall we be adorned and nourished in the lower part of our human nature. In this sublime gift of the Sacrament He also gives us His Spirit full of glory, and the richer gifts of virtues and unspeakable mercies of charity and goodness.

By these we are nourished and adorned and enlightened in the unity of our spirit and in our higher powers, because Christ with all His riches dwells within us.

In the sacrament of the altar He further bestows upon us His sublime personality and His incomprehensible light. Through this we are united and given up to the Father, and the Father receives His elect children at the same time as His only begotten Son, and so we reach our divine inheritance and our eternal felicity.

If a man has diligently considered these things, he will meet Christ in the same way in which Christ comes to him. He will rise to receive Christ with eager joy in his heart, his desires, his love, and all his powers. And it is thus that Christ Himself receives. This joy cannot possibly be too great, for our nature receives His nature, the glorified humanity of Christ, full of gladness and merit. Therefore I desire that in thus receiving man shall, as it were, dissolve and flow forth through his desires, his joys, and his pleasures, for he receives the most lovely, the most gracious, and the kindest of the children of men, and is made one with Him. In this union and this joy great delights often come to men, and many mysterious and secret marvels of divine treasures are manifested and revealed. When in so receiving a man meditates on the torment and the sufferings of this precious body of Christ of which he is partaking, there sometimes enters into him a devotion so loving and a compassion so keen that he desires to be nailed with Christ to the wood of the Cross, and to shed his heart's blood in honour of Christ. And he presses into the wounds and into the open heart of Christ his Saviour. In such exercises revelations and great benefits have often come to men.

The Soul's Hunger for God

Here there begins an eternal hunger, which shall nevermore be satisfied. It is the yearning and the inward aspiration of our faculty of love, and of our created spirit towards an uncreated good. And as the spirit desires joy, and is invited and constrained by God to partake of it, it is always longing to realise joy. Behold then the beginning of an eternal aspiration and of eternal efforts, while our impotence is likewise eternal. These are the poorest of all men, for they are eager and greedy, and they can never be satisfied. Whatever they eat or drink, they can never have enough, for this hunger lasts continually. For a created vessel cannot contain an uncreated good, and hence that continual struggle of the hungry soul, and its feebleness which is swallowed up in God. There are here great banquets of food and drink, which none knoweth saving he who partakes of them; but full satisfaction of joy is the food which is ever lacking, and so the hunger is perpetually renewed. Yet streams of honey flow within reach, full of all delights, for the spirit tastes these pleasures in every imaginable way, but always according to its creaturely nature and below God, and that is why the hunger and the impatience are without end. If God were to grant to this man all the gifts which are possessed by all the saints, and everything that He has to offer, but were to deny Himself, the open-mouthed eagerness of his spirit would be still hungry and unsatisfied. Emotion and the inward contact with God are the explanation of our hunger and our striving; for the Spirit of God gives chase to our spirit, and the closer the contact the greater the hunger and the striving. This is the life of love in its highest development, above reason and higher than all understanding; for in such love reason can neither give nor take away, for our love is in touch with the divine love. And I think that once this point is reached there will be no more separation from God. The contact of God with us, so long as we feel it, and our own loving efforts, are both created and of the nature of the creature, and so they may grow and increase all the days of our life.

The Labour and Rest of Love

In one single moment and at the same time, love labours and rests in its beloved. And the one is strengthened by the other; for the loftier the love, the greater is the rest, and the greater the rest, the closer is the love; for the one lives in the other, and he who loves not rests not, neither does he who rests not know aught of love. There are, nevertheless, some righteous men who believe that they neither love nor rest in God. But this thought itself springs from love, and because their desire to love is greater than their ability, therefore it seems to them that they are powerless to love. And in this labour they taste of love and rest, for none except the resigned, passive, and enlightened man can understand how one may rest and also enjoy.

THE CHRISTIAN LIFE

He (the believer) is hungry and thirsty, for he sees the food of angels and the drink of heaven. He labours diligently in love, for he beholds his rest. He is a pilgrim, and he sees his fatherland. He strives in love for the victory, for he sees his crown. Consolation, peace, joy, beauty, and riches, and all that the heart can desire, are shown to the reason which is enlightened to see God in spiritual similitudes and without measure or limit.... Those who do not possess, at the same time, the power of rest and action, and are not exercised in both, have not received this righteousness of the just.

The Coming of the Bridegroom

What is this eternal coming of our Bridegroom? It is a new birth and a new illumination which are without interruption; for the source from which the brightness streams, and which is itself the brightness, is living and fertile; and so the manifestation of the eternal light is renewed without interruption, in the secret depths of the spirit.... And the coming of the Bridegroom is so swift that He is always coming, and that He dwells within us with His unfathomable riches, and that He returns ever anew in person, with such new brightness that it seems as if He had never come before. For His coming is comprised beyond all limit of time, in an eternal *Now*; and He is ever received with new desires and a new delight. Behold, the joys and the pleasures which this Bridegroom brings with Him at His coming are boundless and without limit, for they are Himself. And this is why the eyes of the spirit, by which the loving soul beholds its Bridegroom, are opened so wide that they will never shut again. For the contemplation and the fixed gaze of the spirit are eternal in the secret manifestation of God. And the comprehension of the spirit is so widely opened, as it waits for the appearance of the Bridegroom, that the spirit itself becomes vast as that which it comprehends. And so is God beheld and understood by God, in whom all our blessedness is found.

THE END

Reviews of precedent Editions

"This volume is a collection of brief but pregnant chapters, written in sweet, simple English which is full of consolation and drops gently into the reader's heart. We give the book our warm commendation and believe that it has a mission of comfort to perform for burdened souls."—*New York Independent.*

" It is pre-eminently a book to put into the hands of the refined, sensitive, scholarly, and devout, when they feel the awful pressure of the greatest bereavement." —*Methodist Times.*

"It is not possible to review such a book as this. Words about it do not tell us what it is. Nor will a selection of words from it half convey its incommunicable fragrance."—*Expository Times.*

Copyright © 2023 by Alicia EDITIONS
Credits: Alicia EDITIONS ; www.canva.com ;
https://commons.wikimedia.org/
wiki/Category:Maurice_Maeterlinck?uselang=fr#/media/File:
Maurice_Maeterlinck's_Signature.jpg
Maurice Maeterlinck's Signature.jpg
https://commons.wikimedia.org/
wiki/File:Antony_van_der_Does_-_The_Mystic_Jan_
van_Ruysbroek.jpg?uselang=fr
File:Antony van der Does - The Mystic Jan van Ruysbroek.jpg - Rijksmuseum
All rights reserved.
No part of this book may be reproduced in any form or by any electronic or mechanical means, including information storage and retrieval systems, without written permission from the author, except for the use of brief quotations in a book review.
ISBN PAPERBACK: 9782384551521
ISBN EBOOK: 9782384551538
ISBN HARDBACK: 9782384551545

www.ingramcontent.com/pod-product-compliance
Lightning Source LLC
LaVergne TN
LVHW032012070526
838202LV00059B/6424